REGROW
YOUR VEGGIES

Regrow Your Veggies

CompanionHouse Books™ is an imprint of Fox Chapel Publishing.

Project Team
Editorial Director: Kerry Bogert
Editor: Chris Cavanaugh
Copy Editor: Katie Ocasio
Design: Mary Ann Kahn
Index: Elizabeth Walker
Translator: Ian Kahn

Originally Published in German as *Regrow Your Veggies* © 2018 by Eugen Ulmer KG, Stuttgart, Germany

ISBN 978-1-62008-368-0

Library of Congress Control Number: 2020942659

This book has been published with the intent to provide accurate and authoritative information in regard to the subject matter within. While every precaution has been taken in the preparation of this book, the author and publisher expressly disclaim any responsibility for any errors, omissions, or adverse effects arising from the use or application of the information contained herein.

Fox Chapel Publishing
903 Square Street
Mount Joy, PA 17552

www.facebook.com/companionhousebooks

We are always looking for talented authors. To submit an idea, please send a brief inquiry to acquisitions@foxchapelpublishing.com.

Printed and bound in China
Fifth printing

Melissa Raupach | Felix Lill

REGROW YOUR VEGGIES

Growing Vegetables from Roots, Cuttings, and Scraps

CONTENTS

CARE INSTRUCTIONS: HOW PLANTS GROW   17

FOREWORD

The good old saying "nothing lasts forever" is especially true when it comes to eating and drinking the things we enjoy. In the stages between childhood and adulthood, our taste buds seem to readjust themselves quite often. People in this stage begin to focus not only on enjoyment, but also health and nutrition.

For me, it was a mix both of all these factors. As a child, my favorite foods varied from spaghetti with store-bought tomato sauce (my parents just couldn't get me to like their homemade version), to pepperoni pizza, and hot dogs from a certain well-known Swedish furniture store. Today, my diet looks a little different. I no longer eat some of my previously beloved foods, like meat, fish, dairy, and eggs. That's right—I'm vegan.

About four years ago, I started becoming more and more interested in nutrition. In my research, I came across, among other things, vegan blogs with incredibly delicious-looking dishes. My love for vegetables used to be limited, so many of these recipes seemed quite exotic at first. But since Curiosity is my middle name, so I cooked and experimented with everything I saw. Eventually, I came to face my biggest opponent: broccoli.

On a list of my least favorite vegetables, broccoli was the undisputed leader. Its smell and green color repelled my inner child. This totally unfounded aversion toward broccoli when I was young resulted in me never even trying it—until four years ago. This story is probably hard to believe now, being the big broccoli fan that I am today. And the moral of the story? Old assumptions (no matter if they're about yourself or somebody else) should always be revisited. You might surprise yourself with what you discover.

Not only have the "traditional" aspects of eating habits ("I've never liked the XY diet!") influenced my culinary journey, but also learning to understand food and ingredients have

Fresh air and regional
vegetables—what
more could you want?

turned a young vegetable hater into an adult veggie fan.

After I switched my diet more and more toward plant-based foods, I slowly became interested in growing my own. My role model in this adventure was my grandmother. One of my earliest memories is of her small garden, where she grew the most delicious tomatoes in the world (I'm probably biased, but they truly were not even close to the kind you would find in a supermarket). I longed to have a garden as glorious as hers, but if you live in the middle of a big city like I do and can't have your own garden, you have to find an alternative solution. Aromatic herbs had become regulars on my shopping list, so my green thumb initially began from simply growing my own herbs. The disposable pots from the supermarket only last for very short time and then wind up in the garbage. Sustainability? Yeah, right! With tasty basil, mint, and rosemary, my regrow project began to blossom. Over time, home-grown lettuce and other vegetables like tomatoes and radishes found a home on my little balcony.

Self-cultivation, plant diversity, etc. fascinated me, and in 2013, I became aware of the trend of "regrowing" via

Fruits and vegetables are essential for a balanced and healthy diet.

social media videos and blog posts. Equally skeptical and intrigued ("How could this possibly work?"), I began my first attempt at regrowing vegetables on the windowsill in my home. My initial skepticism evaporated when I noticed the results of my little flower pot: it worked!

Ever since then I have been fascinated in "regrowing." In this book, I would like to share my knowledge, my personal experiences, as well as tips and suggestions. What motivates me?

1 Producing your own food:
Contrary to popular belief, you don't actually need a whole garden to grow your own vegetables. All you need is a small flower pot to make your regrow dreams a reality! This is not only great news for adult city dwellers like myself, but also for kids to experience growing healthy food firsthand.

2 Note: Whether in cookbooks or in online recipes, exotic plants from all over the world seem to suppress local cuisine, but try to keep your garden simple. There are so many types of vegetables and fruits that grow locally, taste delicious, and can be integrated into many different recipes (even fancy ones). Regrowing vegetables shouldn't be complicated.

3 Sustainability and recycling:
These things are very important in our modern garbage-producing societies. We have a responsibility to take care of our planet and preserve its beauty for future generations. This can only happen if the world comes together to do something about our waste problem. Each and every person can contribute to achieving this goal.

4 Fun and curiosity: Last but not least, regrowing should be fun! After all, what's better than watching plants grow (literally) and getting to taste the results? Regrowing is not only a special treat for children, but it also teaches them an important lesson: that food doesn't just come from a grocery store.

The following chapter is dedicated entirely to sustainability because this aspect of regrowing is the closest to my heart.

After that, we'll dive into helpful care tips and detailed regrow instructions for delicious fruits, vegetables, and herbs. Finally, you'll learn what to do if problems arise so that your regrow projects can be a tasty success.

Have fun regrowing!
Melissa Raupach

SUSTAINABILITY AND RECYCLING

This aspect of regrowing is of great moral importance to me. By regrowing your vegetables, you're contributing to the sustainability of the planet, and the best part is that anyone can do it.

Living in a globalized world has many advantages. Of course, transporting people and goods is much quicker, but also knowledge, culture, and other perspectives cross borders more easily than anyone could have imagined a few decades ago. With all the advantages that globalization brings developed countries and its citizens, it's also important to consider its negative effects. Unfortunately, the mantra of "higher, further, faster" often comes at the expense of humans, animals, and the environment. Even though globalization is irreversible, it is not (yet!) set in stone how we humans in industrialized nations will pave the way for the future. Taking care of our planet and its resources is, in my eyes, one of the greatest challenges of today's generations.

Even if that sounds like a ton of responsibility at first, anybody can contribute their part by living a more sustainable lifestyle. Hardly any other thing out there lends itself better to this goal than changing personal consumption behavior. Whether it's the clothes you wear or the electronic devices you use, Our purchasing behavior influences both supply and demand. An example of this is the increasing number of vegan and vegetarian products in supermarkets, cookbooks, and restaurants. It's not

In more and more cities, it is becoming possible to shop in package-free stores.

Not only can vegetables be recycled, but their containers as well.

about giving something up, but about consciously choosing to consume more sustainable products.

Another important issue that is closely related to our consumer behavior is the garbage it produces. In a recent study, a whopping yearly average of 940 pounds (426kg) of household waste (and not including large items like electronics) were measured—way too much! Making a conscious decision in this regard can also really make a difference.

One way, for example, is by recycling. Much of what is carelessly thrown in the garbage can be used reused. From pickle jars to shoe boxes, with a bit of creativity and ingenuity,

Fresh local fruits and vegetables not only taste better, but they're also better for the environment.

these objects can be given a new life; not to mention, it saves you money. With the internet and many social media channels full of do-it-yourself inspiration, those of us who aren't as creative can easily find very detailed instructions on being better recyclers. Recycling can, therefore, be seen as the alternative to a "disposable" lifestyle—and the same can be said of regrowing unused vegetables.

By regrowing, you're reducing household waste and providing fresh food at the same time. You probably won't be able to replace your entire produce consumption with regrown vegetables (unless you don't eat a lot of vegetables or you're a real regrow pro). But that's not the goal. Rather, it's about returning to simplicity.

This is closely related to the current "zero waste" trend. This global movement doesn't just recycle waste, but attempts to avoid it altogether. The principles of zero waste are known as the five Rs: refuse, reduce, reuse, recycle, and rot.

Some of the zero waste pioneers out there produce in a whole year only enough waste to fit inside a small jam jar. Although you can't make such an extreme change overnight, it is still a good idea to pay attention to your consumption habits and reduce waste wherever possible. By regrowing vegetable waste, vegetables are not only reused, but organic waste, and the carbon footprint associated with transporting it in garbage trucks, is reduced. Creating a new life out of organic waste is a return to the natural circle of life. Aside from the ethical motivations, it's also a lot of fun to hone your skills as a regrow gardener.

CARE INSTRUCTIONS: HOW PLANTS GROW

Plants can't be lumped into one category: some plants love to be in the sun while others prefer the shade. The wide variety of plants requires gardeners to pay close attention to their plants' needs. So, let's start with a few of the basics of plant propagation and care.

On the following pages, you'll learn everything you need to know about vegetative propagation. This is the name of the process behind regrowing plants. Additionally, you'll learn where to place your plants and how to care for them during cultivation: from watering to fertilization and overwintering.

VEGETATIVE PROPAGATION: TURNING ONE INTO MANY

When regrowing plants, you have to distinguish between generative and vegetative propagation. Both types occur naturally in nature and play a role in regrowing: however, for most of the regrow techniques in this book, we'll be using the vegetative propagation method.

Plants primarily use their seeds to create the next generation. Pollen (the "male," if you will), comes in contact with the stigma (the "female"). This process is called generative or sexual reproduction in plants. Vegetation like avocados and mangoes (whose regrow instructions are also in this book) grow out of their seeds and are, therefore, generative.

When plants reproduce without seeds, it is called vegetative propagation. Using discarded parts of vegetables to grow new ones falls into this type of plant reproduction. Vegetative propagation works very differently than generative propagation. Since a part of the mother plant is used to grow a new plant from it, this process is known as asexual reproduction. Those

reading carefully may have noticed a key distinction: the mother plant and the offspring have the same genes because the mother is able to create offspring without fertilization. Therefore, the regrown plants are direct clones of the mother plant. But don't worry, Your house isn't going to turn into the set of a science fiction movie. For plants in the wild, this process of propagation happens naturally every day. Still, it might sound strange to clone your vegetables for fun because this would be morally unimaginable for animals and humans (and rightfully so).

Many green thumbs have been using this method of vegetative propagation for a long time. The concept is pretty interesting: Let's say you have a favorite plant in your garden that bears perfect fruit. With vegetative

1

2

3

propagation, you can make a perfect clone of it with the exact same characteristics.

The asexual form of reproduction is a true miracle of nature. Isn't it crazy to think that you can cut off a piece of a vegetable and grow an entirely new one from it? This is possible because each individual plant cell contains all of its genetic material. That means, for example, that a cell in a stalk of romaine lettuce has the same amount of genetic information as a cell from its roots or leaves. The technical term for this is *totipotent*.

With regrowing, the cells reprogram themselves to take on new roles inside the plant. This process is what enables regrowing to work. The reprogramming of cells works especially well with young and fresh plants. Consider this when choosing your regrow veggies.

In order to successfully regrow your vegetables, you should know a bit about plant care. You will learn more about this on the following pages.

LOCATION

The first thing to consider to ensure successful regrowing is, of course, location. Just as we humans are different, plants have different needs that must be satisfied.

Light

The sun is the key to life: This is the first thing you hear in biology class when learning about photosynthesis. Plants generate energy via a chemical process that turns energy from the sun (solar energy) into energy in the form of sugar that plants can use. Light does not only determine if a plant will be able to survive. It also affects how the plant grows. In general, plants prefer one of three types of light: sun, partial sun, or shade. It is important that you give your plant what it wants; otherwise, you'll just make it harder for the plant to grow and bear fruit for you. It must also be noted that the hours of sunlight a plant gets is only partially important. More important is whether a plant is getting bright sunlight from morning to midday or during the afternoon. This affects the intensity of the light, which you may have noticed yourself while sunbathing. In a nutshell: know what light your plant likes!

Light is especially important when your regrow plants begin to establish their roots. Because of this, spring and early summer are generally the best times of year for regrowing. However, outside of these light-intensive months, it is still possible to regrow plants. Deep into winter, you may need to use artificial light sources if natural light isn't enough. These days, you can find special LED plant lights that are not only effective because of their optimized light spectrum, but are also very energy efficient. In this book, you will see a small info box ("regrow-check") letting you know the light requirements for each plant. Follow the provided information to find a suitable place for your plants to grow to their full potential.

Warmth

If I were a plant, I'd probably be one who grows best in the Southern region. Whenever I'm on vacation in a warm part of the world, I feel

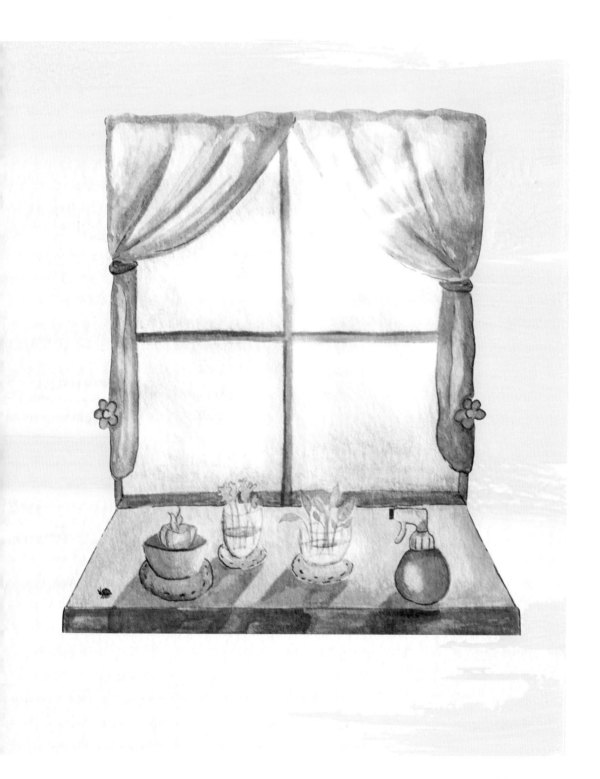

healthy and happy. For many plants it's the same. Warmth is also a form of energy and helps many types of plants grow. As you can imagine, a plant's origin as well as where it grows are indicators of its preferred climate. Exotic fruits like mangoes and bananas prefer warm, humid tropical climates. Other regrow veggies, like the Jerusalem artichoke, don't have any maximum temperature requirements. The optimal warmth for each plant is specified in the regrow instructions. As a rule of thumb, 60°F (20°C) is an acceptable temperature for most plants.

NO COLD FEET!

Warmth is especially important in the roots of your plants. There are special heating mats available to to support and even accelerate root growth. This is a very useful investment for serious regrowers.

Soil

A pot or flower bed with soil is like a house for our plants. Soil quality effects the health of its residents. For this reason, don't cut corners when it comes to potting and planting materials. Invest in high-quality soil—this will make your regrow seedling happy and healthy. You can find special potting compost for cuttings in garden centers, nurseries, or online (a cutting is the name of the piece of a plant which is used for regrowing).

Potting compost is especially useful for starting the regrowing process, and is characterized by the fact that it is very permeable to water. This helps avoid the risk of waterlogging. Another advantage of this soil is that it is low in nutrients. This may sound like a disadvantage at first, but it is the key to strong root growth. Because of the lack of nutrients, the plant creates bigger roots in order to seek out more nutrients. However, you shouldn't leave your plant in the compost soil forever. Once the plant has started to grow and has developed strong roots, it's best to then transfer it to regular soil. Organic peat-free soil works particularly well. Using organic soil goes along with the goal of sustainability as well.

CARE

Location is not the only important factor for your plantlets. The right care will determine the success or failure of your regrow attempts. Give your plants love and attention! They will thank you for it with a rich yield and remarkable growth.

Water

Just like the sun, water is a key to all life on earth. Perhaps you've forgotten to water a plant at some point in your life. The result was probably a dried-up, withered mess.

Watering regularly is also an important part of regrowing your vegetables. There are generally two strategies when it comes to regrowing: place the stalk directly into water or into damp soil. Either way, water is key. Vegetables and herbs that spend some time in a glass of water before they're planted relish in the fresh H20. Stagnant water can start to get musty after just a few days, so it's best to change the water daily. This is also good for the plant stalks because stagnant water increases the chance of rot at the location where the plant was cut.

Some vegetables and herbs, however, should never be placed in water. Onions, for example, should go right into soil! You shouldn't leave other plants in water for too long: In water, plants develop roots suitable for that environment. Once they are transferred to soil, they need different roots in order to absorb its nutrients. Don't listen to advice (especially from questionable Internet sources) claiming you can leave plants in water permanently without needing to pot them; it's just not true.

After you have potted your plant, water still remains an important factor in your regrow success. Immediately after moving your plant

Water is vital—even for mint. But after a few days, they also belong in soil.

GREENHOUSE

To ensure high humidity, you can buy a mini greenhouse. They can be found in many stores as well as online.

You can also punch holes in a freezer bag and stretch it over the plant, or place a large cut-off plastic bottle around it.

If the water can't drain properly, the plants get waterlogged, which is very counterproductive to their growth. It increases the risk of rot and other plant diseases. By the way, The amount of water each regrow plant needs is listed in the Regrow-Check info bars, as well.

Humidity

Water in the soil isn't the only moisture your plants need. The air also plays an important role. The plants' pores open depending on the humidity of their surroundings. This regulates the process of photosynthesis. Again, different types of plants have different humidity

to soil, water it generously—ideally with rain water (if you have some available at home).

Plants need cool water in order to absorb nutrients out of the soil and distribute them throughout the organism, which helps them grow. As you can see, watering is vital for your little green friends. If the roots don't get enough water, it causes stress in the plants—you would probably have the same reaction if you didn't get enough to drink. When stressed, the plants go into survival mode—they don't use any strength or energy in growing, blossoming, or producing fruit. So, for a successful yield, remember to water your plants!

But this does not mean that you should drown your plants either. Most plants do not handle that very well.

requirements. While one may love dry air, others prefer it warm and humid (especially plants that come from tropical regions).

Because small young plants have barely any roots at first, it is harder for them to absorb nutrients from soil. Proper humidity is, therefore, veryimportant at this stage. This reduces water evaporation in the plants.

Repotting

After a while, it makes sense to repot your plant. There are several reasons for this. On the one hand, you supply the fresh nutrients with new soil. On the other hand, a larger pot encourages the plant to grow more and has a positive effect on its strength and general health. But don't go overboard when selecting the size of the new pot. As a rule of thumb, choose a pot that is 2–4in (5–10cm) larger in diameter than the old one. That's enough room for one year (or longer).

The beetroot is looking forward to its new, nutrient-rich soil to continue to grow.

When repotting, feel free to get creative: many old containers make great hip flower pots.

Make sure to use high-quality soil for your plants—they will thank you for it.

If you're wondering how to tell if your plant needs to be repotted: Just take a look at the roots. If the roots are developing toward the bottom of the pot and you can see sprouting, it's time for a bigger pot—your little plant will appreciate it.

The best time for repotting, according to gardening experts, is in the early spring, when the increased light and warm temperatures help the plant settle into its new home and grow. Since your regrow plants will generally spend all their time indoors, you can repot them at any time of year. After repotting, it is important (like with the first planting) that the plant receives plenty of water.

Fertilizing

To ensure a good supply of nutrients, you should regularly fertilize your regrow vegetables—but not too much. A thimble full of plant-based fertilizer once every two weeks is sufficient. You can also use special vegetable fertilizer. Because the potting soil isn't very rich in nutrients, don't forget to fertilize the normal soil after repotting – but you only need to do this for two to three weeks after repotting. This is how long it takes for plants to root into the new soil.

Overwintering

When the days get shorter and the weather gets colder, you might wonder how winter effects your regrow projects. With reduced daylight and colder temperatures, your plants will also notice that winter has begun.

Again, plants differ in their relationship with winter: local vegetables fare much better in cooler temperature than those from exotic regions. Since most of your regrow plants will be inside your home, where it's warm all year round, this shouldn't be an issue. Just make sure that the air in your home isn't too dry. As mentioned earlier, the amount of water in the air (humidity) is important for the health of your plants.

The instructions include a note for all regrow plants that require special care during the winter months.

Now that you're familiar with the basics of plant care, we can start with the regrow instructions. The following are sorted by vegetables, herbs, and fruit.

REGROW INSTRUCTIONS

In this chapter, you will learn how to harvest and use your regrow plants. In the regrow check at the end of the instructions for each vegetable you'll find the most important information: how bright, how warm, how humid does your new roommate prefer its surroundings—more stars mean more light, warmth, and humidity are required. This chart also shows how difficult each project is—this is especially relevant for regrow newcomers.

REGROW-CHECK

Light:
Shady ***** Sunny

Warmth:
Rather cool ***** Nice and warm

Humidity:
Rather dry ***** Keep nice and moist

Difficulty:
Very easy ***** Experience or patience needed

CHINESE CABBAGE

➡ Quiz: Where is Chinese cabbage from? Okay, you got me: The answer is obvious. Even though Chinese cabbage (also called Napa cabbage) originated in China, it has been used in Japanese and Korean cuisine for hundreds of years.

Other common names for this member of the cabbage family are Peking cabbage or Japanese cabbage. You might also hear it referred to as celery cabbage. In the past century, this special type of cabbage has made its way west. You've probably seen it on your plate at a Chinese restaurant, or maybe you enjoy cooking with it at home.

How Chinese cabbage came to exist remains a mystery to this day. Apparently, this cabbage is a cross between the turnip and bok choy. It is often confused for the latter. Compared to its presumed father, however, the Chinese cabbage forms solid heads that are cylinder shaped. The leaves mostly range from white to light green. There are also darker varieties, however.

It is rich in vitamin A and C; you can also find calcium, iron, and magnesium in its mild tasting laves. No need to worry about counting calories here: with only 12kcal per 3½oz (100g), it has less calories than celery.

Regrowing Chinese cabbage is very simple. You won't be able to regrow a whole head, but you will be able to grow new leaves. So, what are you waiting for? By regrowing Chinese cabbage, you can bring part of the Far East right into your own home.

REGROW YOUR CHINESE CABBAGE

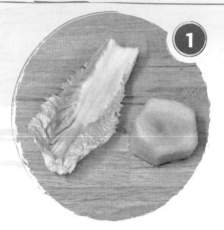

1 Cut off a generous amount of the Chinese cabbage stem and prepare it as follows: The base should be at least 1.5 x 1.5in (4 x 4cm) in size. The recommended height is 1in (3cm). After slicing and dicing, you should be left with a Chinese cabbage cube.

2 Now the water comes into play. Be careful: please don't drown your Chinese cabbage. Instead, make sure the bottom is mostly submerged in water—this makes it easier for the plant to grow. You should change the water regularly: about once every two to three days. A bright window, balcony or patio is a good location for growing. Because Chinese cabbage likes the sun.

3 At this point, opinions tend to vary: You can either leave the stem in the water and continue to provide fresh H_2O or you can remove it and plant it in a container of your choice after seven to ten days. I highly recommend the latter. After two to three weeks, you will start to see the first leaves sprout. These you can harvest.

HARVESTING AND USE

As mentioned already: Don't expect a complete head of Chinese cabbage on your windowsill! Instead, tasty cabbage leave will grow out of the stem which are a great ingredient for many dishes. Cut off the leaves close to the stem. Make sure you are using a clean knife. Making cuts with a dirty knife are a gateway for all kinds of bacteria. So, to be on the safe side, make sure everything is clean.

After harvesting, you'll have tender leaves that taste pleasantly mild. Even non-cabbage fans will enjoy them—I promise! You can use the leaves raw or cooked. I definitely wouldn't cook them all the way through, however, because this would cause them to lose their satisfying crunch.

Chinese cabbage is a staple of Asian cuisine—from wok dishes to soups and salads. Maybe you already know it in the form of Korean sauerkraut, also known as kimchi. It's usually spicy and I can

absolutely recommend it. You can find plenty of kimchi recipes and instructions online. It's worth a shot, right?

Chinese cabbage is becoming more and more popular in the US and in Europe. The amount of space being used for cultivation continues to grow. Lovers of Asian cuisine (like me) are very happy about this. That being said, it's not very difficult to regrow delicious Chinese cabbage leaves in your own home.

REGROW-CHECK

Light ✳✳✳
Warmth ✳✳
Humidity ✳✳✳✳
Difficulty ✳✳✳

SCALLIONS

Scallions are also known as Spring onion and leek onion. The botanical name for it is *Allium fistulosum*. It belongs to the same plant family as onions, leeks, and garlic.

The native region of scallions is likely in the the Far East. From there, its origins spread to west and to the east. It is said to have been growing in China for over 2000 years. It's no newcomer to Europe either. Above all, it is very strongly represented in Asian regions as an integral part of many dishes. There, the plant is more reminiscent of thick chives, while the North American and European variety is known for its typical tube shape. Along with shape, there are a few other differences across the regional varieties: spiciness and color, for example. Some varieties even have a red color.

Generally, you can use the scallions where you would otherwise use a normal yellow onion. The longer, greener scallion, however, has a much milder taste. It's perfect for people who find the taste of a regular onion too strong.

When it comes to regrowing, scallions are the perfect starter-vegetable. It is easy to grow and unlikely to fail.

✳

Scallions are the perfect regrow vegetables for impatient people since they grow very fast and can be used for all kinds of recipes. So next time, don't throw away the roots of your scallions—give them a new life instead!

REGROW YOUR SCALLIONS

1 Cut off the root end of the scallion so that you have a piece about 2in (5cm) long. Be very careful with the roots. The healthier and more intact they are, the faster they will grow.

2 Now it's time for a long bath in fresh room-temperature water. Let the root pieces sit in a glass jar for three to five days. A bright spot is the ideal location. Change the water every day or two.

3 After a few days in the water, you should notice the first signs of rooting. Now you can plant the scallion in soil. The roots should be well covered. Again, a bright location is perfect in this stage. Make sure it gets enough water. Soon, your scallion will sprout and greet you with its green stems.

HARVESTING AND USE

The harvesting process is similar to the previous regrowing project. Once the stems have regrown significantly, you can cut off as much as you need (with a clean and sharp knife, of course) and leave the rest in the soil. You can also take the entire scallion out of the soil and eat the whole thing.

Scallions are versatile and can be used in many dishes. I like using them as a spicy crunchy ingredient in salads. Also, in many Asian dishes, this green plant lends plenty of flavor. You should make sure to add scallions to your recipes near the end of cooking or sautéing. If you add them too early, they will lose their crunchiness and become floppy.

THE SCALLION: A WATER PLANT?

There are a couple of websites on the Internet that recommend skipping the step of planting the scallion in soil. With this technique, the scallion just sits a glass of water to regrow. This process does work, but the scallion loses a lot of its taste and flavor intensity. This is because the plant can't get enough necessary nutrients from the soil. But if you want to give it a try, go for it.

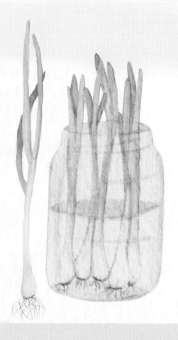

REGROW-CHECK

Light ✲✲✲
Warmth ✲✲
Humidity ✲✲✲
Difficulty ✲

POTATOES

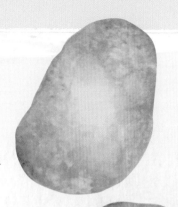

➡ The potato is an ingredient in so many classic recipes around the world. Its homeland is in South America.

Adaptability is one of the potato's great strengths. It is why you can find them all over the world today. China is the world's largest potato grower, followed by India and Russia. The United States is fifth largest, Canada is the eighteenth. The potato is essential in feeding the earth's population—a true staple food rich in vitamins and minerals.

On the island of Chiloé in Chile, traces of wild potato were discovered whose existence could be traced back 13,000 years. Unbelievable, right? On the slopes of the Andes mountains, indigenous people have long been cultivating these nutritious spuds. The true home of the potato (or *papa*, as the locals call it) is Peru with an incredible amount of varieties. Unfortunately, many of these potatoes are endangered, so much so that Peru founded the International Potato Center (IPC) to try to preserve them.

In Europe, this member of the nightshade family arrived in the 16th century, presumably via the Canary Islands. In the areas of today's federal republic of Germany, people were very skeptical about the plant. According to legend, Frederick II of Prussia had to come up with a cunning plan to change their minds. He had soldiers guard his potato fields, which piqued the interest of the surrounding farmers. What was so great about this plant that it needed to be guarded by soldiers? The intrigued farmers snuck onto his fields at night and stole some of the plants to grow for themselves. The soldiers, of course, had been ordered not to intervene with this royal theft. Soon, everyone was talking about the potato.

REGROW YOUR POTATOES

1 In general, you should start regrowing potatoes between January and March. After mid-May, where it can still get pretty cold occasionally, the small spuds can come outside. If the potatoes are a bit on the older side when you plant them, that's ideal. Can you already see its so-called eyes? Perfect! (The eyes are the spots where the potato forms its sprouts.) Instead of throwing away old potatoes, you should regrow them! You can just cut the potato into two parts. Each piece should have at least two eyes to be able to grow roots. Let the potato dry out—so definitely don't put it in water! It can take a few days until it's completely dried out, depending on the humidity in the air. If you can't feel any more moisture at the spot where the potato was cut, it's ready for the next step.

2 Now the potato gets planted. Make sure to choose a large container. Go ahead and get creative: Why not repurpose an antique bathtub? The individual pieces should be placed as deep as possible in the soil and be completely covered. It's important that the soil around the potato is loose enough for the shoots to push through it.

3 After a few months (potatoes need a whole season), you can start harvesting.

HARVESTING AND USE

Potatoes are ripe when the plant begins to die at the surface of the soil. Harvesting your own small potatoes isn't so simple. Being gentle is important. Gently lift the potato plants to loosen the soil around them. Then you can pick the potato out of the root system. Since some of the small spuds may have already fallen off, run your hands through the soil to check.

With your regrow harvest, you can now prepare all types of potato dishes. For me, there's nothing better than rosemary potatoes in the oven. First, thoroughly wash the potatoes (you don't need to peel them but you can). Then halve or cut them into quarters, depending on how big they are, and spread them out on a baking sheet. Season with olive oil, salt, pepper, and rosemary. Bake for 30 to 40 minutes and you have perfectly seasoned potatoes. I also eat boiled potatoes with vegan dips like guacamole or homemade eggplant puree a few times a month.

REGROW-CHECK

Light ✱✱✱✱
Warmth ✱✱
Humidity ✱✱
Difficulty ✱✱✱

LEEKS

Leeks probably wouldn't be at the top of most people's favorite vegetables list. Nevertheless, this green vegetable has a delightfully mild flavor—and is good for more than just soups. It is, however, a proud member of the standard soup greens.

Leeks belong to the allium species. Garlic and onions also belong to this species, although they have a much more intense flavor.

Historically speaking, leeks have been famous for a long time. Some sources believe that humans have been growing them for over 4,000 years. Even murals from the ancient Egyptians prove that leeks had a permanent place on the menu in their time.

The Romans brought leeks to Europe where they spread to the far north of the continent. Supposedly, the emperor Nero (yes, the same emperor who is said to have fiddled while Rome burned) was a big fan of leeks, enough to give him the nickname "porrophagus," or leek-eater. Since Nero wasn't a big fan of jokes at his own expense, this nickname was probably only used behind his back. Do you think Nero was aware that leeks are rich in vitamin K and C? No idea, but along with these vitamins, leeks are also high in beta-carotene.

Whether you're a leek-eater or a leek newbie, the leek is one of the most rewarding vegetables to regrow because it is quick and has a high yield. Additionally, leeks also look great on a window sill, saving you money you might spend on a decorative plant—talk about sustainability!

REGROW YOUR LEEKS

1 Cut off the bottom part of the leek. From the roots to the where it was cut, the stem should measure at least 2in (5cm) in length—a little bit longer is even better. The roots of the leek should already be visible. This means they will be able to grow well.

2 Place the stem in a glass of lukewarm water. The water shouldn't cover the entire stem, but the roots must be completely submerged. The leek will stay here for 5 to 10 days. You should change the water regularly. A bright location is, of course, preferable.

BY THE WAY:

Leeks can be regrown indoors near a window or outside during gardening season.

3 After a week in the water, you should be able to clearly see the roots growing. Now the leek is ready to be planted. The top of the stem should stick out of the surface of the soil, so make sure not to plant the leek too deep. With regular watering, your own regrown leek will emerge from the middle of the stem within a few weeks.

HARVESTING AND USE

To harvest, cut off as much of the leek as you need from the top. If you do this with a sharp and clean knife, it will still continue to grow. This guarantees you an almost unending supply of homegrown leek—except for the flower, which is technically also edible. Plus, your kitchen (or any other room for that matter) can have a nice new houseplant, which otherwise would have been garbage. How great is that!

What you choose to do with your leek is all up to your taste buds. I like leeks in winter soups or as part of a thicker puree. However, on the other hand, in small quantities, they make a great addition to salads and wok dishes. Finally, an absolute hit: leek in a juicy quiche. Doesn't it make your mouth water just thinking about it?

Leek is especially good for people who find the taste of onions or garlic too strong. Its slightly milder flavor is the perfect alternative.

REGROW-CHECK

Light ✳✳✳
Warmth ✳✳
Humidity ✳✳✳✳
Difficulty ✳✳

HORSERADISH

→ If you're a fan of zesty deli sandwiches or enjoy the occasional Bloody Mary, you'll be familiar with horseradish. This spicy root belongs to the cabbage family.

Armoracia rusticana, its scientific name, is originally from southern Europe. There is evidence that it has been used since antiquity. Once it made its way to central Europe, horseradish spread across the continent and now across the world.

Introducing flavor to the often-bland food was not so easy back then—pepper and other spices weren't readily available, not even for kings and royal families. Horseradish became the first common spicy addition to foods, and people fell in love. Even today, this spicy root is an integral part of many cuisines, especially in regions where it is grown.

In some regions of the world, you can still see wild horseradish on the menu. In central Europe, Ukraine, and in western parts of Russia, you might even come across horseradish while walking through nature.

Horseradish is an incredibly robust plant and can survive extremely cold temperatures, withstanding up to -58°F (-50°C)! The leaves do die off in the winter, but the roots (the most important part) still survive.

Regrowing horseradish takes time, but it will give you tasty, spicy roots if you're patient. You can also use the young leaves of the plant for salads, and they can be prepared similarly to spinach.

REGROW YOUR HORSERADISH

1 Cut off the top of the horseradish root. It should be at least 2in (5cm) tall.

2 If it is dried out, it's best to soak it in a jar of fresh lukewarm water. The not-too-cold liquid should cover half of the horseradish for between five and seven days. A bright location is best. You should change the water regularly to prevent it from starting to smell. If the horseradish is fresh, you can plant it in soil right away.

GREEN AND DEVILISHLY SPICY

A distant relative of horseradish is wasabi (*Eutrema japonicum*). It's not called Japanese horseradish for nothing—even if it is significantly spicier than the bright European horseradish. The bright green wasabi (and its often extreme tear-inducing spiciness) is standard in any sushi restaurant. Unlike horseradish, wasabi isn't made from the roots of the plant—its stem is used to create a spicy paste.

3 If you only want to cultivate the leaves, a nice spot near the windowsill will do. To regrow the root, you'll need to give your horseradish more space outdoors in a flower bed. You should begin the regrowing process in spring or early summer. The soil conditions are also important. To keep the root as straight as possible you need loose soil. Now it is time to wait until the horseradish has worked on developing its spicy root this take two whole seasons. The spicy leaves can be harvested sooner.

HARVESTING AND USE

Harvesting regrown horseradish is very simple. The root is fully grown when the leaves above the soil begin to wither. This is a good sign to start harvesting. You can simply pull the roots out of the soil. If you're not ready to eat it yet, you can leave the root in the soil. This doesn't affect the plant.

Freshly harvested horseradish is traditionally paired with hearty foods. Because I don't eat meat or fish, I use it in combination with potato or cabbage dishes. You shouldn't cook horseradish for any reason. It can be cut or grated raw—this is the only way to maintain its spicy flavor.

REGROW-CHECK

Light ✷✷
Warmth ✷✷
Humidity ✷✷✷
Difficulty ✷✷

ROMAINE LETTUCE

Crunchy texture and bright green in color, Romaine lettuce is one of the most common types of lettuce. It belongs to the family of garden greens (*Lactuca sativa*)—which comes as no surprise. As the basis of many salad dishes, it is also, of course, a regrow staple.

Romaine lettuce can be found in various sizes in your local supermarket. Especially popular are romaine hearts. These are the smaller kind and usually come in packs of two or three. The outer leaves are removed, leaving the super crispy romaine heart.

Romaine lettuce is a usual suspect on the regrowing veggies list because it is a very reliable regrower. Additionally, many households regularly throw away the unused parts of this salad component. Now you can kill two birds with one stone.

Originally, like so many other vegetables, romaine lettuce comes from the Mediterranean. Some sources claim it had already been used 4,000 years ago in ancient Egypt. Today, it's a regular in salads in Europe and North America and can be seen in any restaurant (probably because it is also very healthy). One study, which ranked the healthiest fruits and vegetables, put romaine lettuce in ninth place—a very good result.

Depending on how big your regrow container is, you should choose a lettuce stem that won't outgrow it.

REGROW YOUR ROMAINE LETTUCE

1 The next time you're cutting lettuce, don't forget about regrowing! The stem of the romaine lettuce needs to be at least 2in (5cm) long. If it's any shorter, regrowing becomes unnecessarily difficult.

2 Now the stem can be placed in water. Make sure that about half of the stem is submerged. Romaine lettuce also likes a well-lit environment. Choose a bright spot in your house, and replace the water every couple of days. Let the plant stay here for five to ten days.

3 Once the stem starts to grow new roots and the cut-off top of the plant starts to grow, it's time to plant the romaine lettuce. The stem goes into the soil, while the newly emerging leaves stay above the soil. After all, they need light to produce fresh leafy greens.

4 Make sure to keep the soil moist. Within a few weeks, the leaves will get bigger and bigger until they're ready to become part of your next salad.

HARVESTING AND USE

There are a few ways to harvest romaine lettuce. You can harvest the entire head at once by simply cutting off all the leaves above the soil with a sharp knife. Whether or not it will continue to grow depends on how well it is rooted—it's worth a try. The other option is to only remove the leaves that you need at any given time. The lettuce will continue to grow new leaves. I usually use all the leaves at once.

The amount of lettuce recipes is endless—especially online. From classic mixed salads to exotic combinations, anything is possible. Due to its mild taste, romaine lettuce is the perfect companion for many dishes. And, although it may sound odd at first, combining it with fruits like strawberries or nectarines is a real treat. A mix of romaine and other types of

lettuce is also a great idea, especially if your regrow harvest isn't enough for an entire serving.

Another option is to use romaine lettuce as a "food boat." For soups, curries, and rice dishes, you can use the crispy leaves as a kind of vegetable spoon. This is a great way to get kids to eat lettuce.

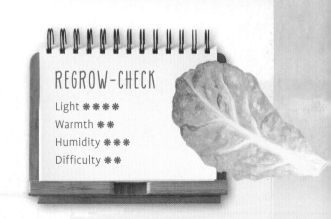

REGROW-CHECK

Light ✹✹✹✹
Warmth ✹✹
Humidity ✹✹✹
Difficulty ✹✹

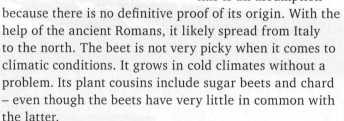

BEETS

Its bright magenta color is its unmistakable trademark. The red beet is polarizing: Either you love its intense earthy flavor or you hate it.

The beet (*Beta vulgaris subspecies vulgaris*) belongs to the Betoideae family. It is a form of turnip. Originally, the beet comes from the Mediterranean. But this is an assumption because there is no definitive proof of its origin. With the help of the ancient Romans, it likely spread from Italy to the north. The beet is not very picky when it comes to climatic conditions. It grows in cold climates without a problem. Its plant cousins include sugar beets and chard – even though the beets have very little in common with the latter.

This classic winter vegetable owes its intense red color to glycoside betanin. Beets have many other benefits as well: rich in vitamin B, iron, potassium, and folic acid, it is high up on the healthiness scale.

Take note, you can also enjoy the leaves of the beet—and this is what we will be regrowing. An entire beet will unfortunately not grow back in most cases. However, there are plenty of uses for the leaves—which you'll soon discover.

REGROW YOUR BEET

1 Cut off the top of the beetroot (i.e., the part that the leaves grow out of). This is essential! Equally important is that you use a raw beet and not the pre-cooked kind from the supermarket. The piece you cut off should be at least 1in (3cm) thick, but not more than a third of the entire beet.

2 Now place the beet stem in water. Make sure that the "head" of the beet is facing upwards. If it is the other way around, no leaves will grow. Then place the glass near a window. Your beet needs sunlight to grow. Change the water once every couple of days, because if you don't, the stem will start to smell. Very fresh, crisp beets can theoretically be placed directly in soil without needing water first.

RED BEET CARPACCIO

Cut cooked beets into very thin slices. Then combine them with cooked beetroot leaves, walnuts, high-quality olive oil, and drizzle with dark balsamic vinegar—the perfect dish to bring to parties.

<u>3</u> If the beet was in water, it should stay in the soil for five to seven days. The "head," from which the leaves will sprout, shouldn't be buried under the soil. Beets like it when the soil is constantly a bit moist (but not too wet, of course). In two to three weeks, the first leaves should be visible.

HARVESTING AND USE

The leaves are harvested by carefully cutting and removing them, and just like that, you have got fresh beetroot leaves. It's advisable to harvest the leaves only if you plan to use them shortly afterward; otherwise, the tender green leaves will quickly start to wilt and stop looking so healthy. But be careful: if you harvest all the leaves at once, the plant may not be able to recover from the shock.

There's a wide variety of recipes for the beet—the vegetable has begun a sort of renaissance in the last few years. There are also many ways to utilize the leaves and integrate them into delicious dishes. For one thing, you can use them raw in salads. I like them best when they're steamed or sautéed. You can prepare them like you would spinach or chard. They make a great topping for many dishes—exotic beetroot soup, for example, is made by mixing potatoes and beets with coconut milk, lemon juice, garlic, salt, and pepper in a soup.

REGROW-CHECK

Light ✱✱✱
Warmth ✱✱
Humidity ✱✱✱
Difficulty ✱✱

CELERY

Celery is definitely one of my favorite vegetables to eat and to regrow. In terms of taste, these crunchy sticks aren't only great in salads, but also make the perfect snack. They go great with hummus or homemade peanut butter.

In the celery family, along with common celery, there is also celeriac and leaf celery. All three belong to the apiaceae family and all come from the same type of wild celery. It's different from the other types of celery because it has a smaller root bulb. The plant grows long strong bright green stems with an intense flavor. That said, common celery is significantly milder then its relatives, and its effect as an ingredient is much more understated.

The Latin name for celery is "*Apium graveolens* var. *dulce*." The meaning of the word "graveolens" has a funny history: in Latin, a rough translation would be "strong smelling."

But taste aside, celery is a leader in nutritious value: 3½oz (100g) only contain 18 calories! The reason for this is that celery is 92% water. Despite this, it's rich in vitamin C and magnesium.

Regrowing this healthy flavor bomb is very simple and very fruitful. How great is that!

REGROW YOUR CELERY

1 Remove the stem of the celery with a sharp knife. The piece should be at least 2in (5cm) long.

2 Place the separated stem in a glass of lukewarm water so that half of the celery is above the surface of the water. Leave it in a bright spot for five to seven days. You should replace the water at least once—because who likes taking a bath in the same water for a whole week? In addition, it's helpful to spray the celery stem regularly with water. You can use a normal household spray bottle.

A TIP FOR MORE HUMIDITY

Instead of using a spray bottle filled with water, you can take a freezer bag, poke small holes in it, and stretch it over the glass with the plant in it. You could also use a mini greenhouse.

3 After a week, you can plant the celery in soil. The stalk should be almost entirely covered by the soil; only the leaves that have begun to grow in the middle should remain above the soil. After six weeks of waiting (and watering!), your celery will be ready for its first harvest.

HARVESTING AND USE

Patience isn't a virtue for nothing—and you'll definitely need it if you want to be a regrower. It will take a few weeks before the celery is ready to be harvested. To regrow enough celery for one person, you'll need to grow 10 to 20 stalks from reused stems, but the tasty, self-grown celery (with its delicious leaves) are worth the wait.

Harvest the plant by cutting off the celery sticks from the stalk with a sharp knife or plucking the leaves by hand. Again, harvest carefully so that the plant can recover and continue to grow!

I enjoy using celery for salads, adding a unique crunch to the mixture. The leaves are also great in salads. They taste best when slightly steamed or sautéed, and are tasty for Asian-style dishes with soy and peanut sauces. Celery is great to eat with dips like hummus or baba ghanoush (a delicious eggplant sesame dip).

REGROW-CHECK

Light ✻✻✻
Warmth ✻✻
Humidity ✻✻✻
Difficulty ✻✻

SWEET POTATOES

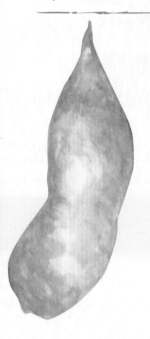

One of my personal favorites in the vegetable aisle is the sweet potato. Its popularity in North America has increased enormously in recent years. It's hard to find a hip burger restaurant in a big city, or even a small-town diner, these days that doesn't have sweet potato fries on the menu.

It's not just the restaurant scene that's taken a liking to this orange-colored spud. They are a standard at most supermarkets these days and thus are in more and more home kitchens.

The sweet potato originates from the tropical and subtropical regions of South America. The indigenous tribes of the area were the first to eat and grow them. They also gave it its name: *batate*. This is also why its scientific name is *Ipomoea batatas*.

The sweet potato made its way to Europe, like many other unknown species at the time, through travelers returning from their faraway adventures with their discoveries from the new world. The sweet potato is said to have arrived in England even before the regular potato, but for reasons unknown today, the Europeans focused solely on the regular potato and the sweet potato was forgotten for a long time. In the US, it was only a staple during the holidays until a few years ago!

Today's hype surrounding this sweet spud can be seen not only in the numerous recipes it contains but also in the amount of people growing and selling it. After centuries of neglecting the sweet potato, we now have to "relearn" how to cultivate them here in our part of the world. The first attempts were quite promising.

Sweet potatoes can absolutely be regrown, but they require some patience.

REGROW YOUR SWEET POTATO

1 In general, you should start regrowing sweet potatoes at home in the months between December and February. This timing is important to allow strong roots to form by autumn. The first step, of course, is to find yourself a sweet potato. As with the potato (page 42), it is advantageous if your sweet potato is a bit older and has already begun to form some of the so-called eyes. This increases the chances of a successful regrow. Next, cut off a 1in (2–3cm) thick section at one end of the potato, preferably with at least one eye.

SPACE EXPEDITION

Since the sweet potato is rich in so many important nutrients and very easy to cultivate, NASA considered it an essential crop for all future space exploration missions. Who knows, maybe it will be the first vegetable to ever land on Mars!

2 Now, the severed piece of sweet potato can either take a water bath or be planted into soil right away. I would usually recommend the latter. If you, however, want to show your kids how roots form, you could definitely put it in water first. If temperatures are warm enough, you should be able to see roots after two weeks. Dry and shriveled pieces can benefit from a water bath of one to two days before being planted in soil.

3 The container for planting should be as large as possible If the container is too small, the roots will not have enough room. A sunny location is as important as watering. Be sure it doesn't get waterlogged. After mid-May, the plant can move outside to the vegetable patch. You can also successfully cultivate sweet potatoes indoors in a flowerpot with a volume of 13gal (50L) or more. This is when you will have to begin exercising patience. It takes an entire season before you can harvest your self-grown sweet potatoes.

HARVESTING AND USE

As you can imagine, it takes a lot of work for this little piece of potato to grow new roots, leaves, and tasty tubers—so it takes a while. You will know that the sweet potato is ready to be harvested when its leaves begin to die. Do this the same way you would with a regular potato (i.e., lift the plant carefully, harvest the sweet potato, and comb through the soil for smaller potatoes).

There is no shortage of sweet potato recipes online. My favorite is homemade sweet potato fries. In autumn and winter, I also love baking entire sweet potatoes in the oven. I slice them in half and fill them with things like guacamole, hummus, or a sauce made from tomatoes, cilantro, corn, and kidney beans. Sweet potatoes are also great for soups and casseroles.

REGROW-CHECK

Light ✴✴✴✴
Warmth ✴✴✴✴
Humidity ✴✴✴
Difficulty ✴✴✴✴

JERUSALEM ARTICHOKES

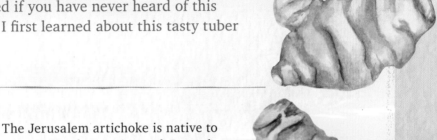

➤ Don't be surprised if you have never heard of this root vegetable. Even I first learned about this tasty tuber just a few years ago.

Although Jerusalem artichoke isn't known very well, it has a wide range of varieties. Some, like the "white truffel" variant, are considered delicacies. Whether you're a gormet foodie or not, everyone should give this root vegetable a try!

The Jerusalem artichoke is native to eastern North America and Central America. The plant likely spread over time from Mexicao northward. The indigenous people were cultivating it long before Columbus had even thought about becoming an explorer. Jerusalem artichoke came to Europe by way of France in the 17th century. They called the unknown vegetable "Indian potato" at the time. Coincidentally, Indians from the Tupinambá tribe were visiting at the time. And this is how it came to be called *topinambour*. There are other names for this root vegetable as well. In places it is called "earth apple" or "earth pear." The name "Jerusalem artichoke" likely has to do with its artichoke-like taste. Botanically speaking, however, this plant belongs to the daisy family.

A very special aspect of the Jerusalem artichoke is its leaves. They look very much like sunflowers—and that's no coincidence. Sunflowers and Jerusalem artichokes are in fact related; they come from the same plant family.

REGROW YOUR JERUSALEM ARTICHOKE

1 Jerusalem artichoke is started indoors (beginning in January) and transplanted outside after mid-May. Cut the Jerusalem artichoke tuber into two roughly equal pieces. It's important that each piece has at least one eye. The plant will later sprout from these eyes. That means: the more eyes, the better.

2 The Jerusalem artichoke pieces don't have to be in water first. However, if the pieces are a bit soft and shriveled, this is a sign that a few days in a water bath is a good idea. This will make them thick and juicy again. If this isn't the case, feel free to place them directly in soil.

THE HEALTHY MIRACLE TUBER

It is rich in fiber, low in calories, and full of calcium, iron, and vitamin B1. With all of thesee benefits in mind, realize it will take quite some time to regrow Jerusalem artichokes.

3 Plant the pieces at least 4in (10cm) deep in a container of your choice. Make sure the pieces have sufficient space between them. Position the pieces so that the eyes are facing upwards. Now it's time to With all of these After a few weeks, you will start to see the first sprouts on the surface. At the beginning of autumn, you will start to see Jerusalem artichokes in your flower bed or planter. Leave a few in the soil so you'll have more to harvest in a year.

HARVESTING AND USE

The artichokes are ripe when the parts of the plant above-ground begin to wither and die. Like with sweet potatoes, this takes at least one entire garden season. Getting the artichokes out of the soil requires a bit of skill. The best way to do it is to loosen the soil and carefully lift the plant. Then you can pick the small tubers from the root system. If you're starting to wonder what you can do with your new root vegetable, wonder no more!

I prefer oven-baked Jerulsalem artichokes. After cleaning the tubers, cut them up and coat them with olive oil, salt, pepper, and spices. Then place them in the oven. This is the perfect side dish for salads and vegetable stews like ratatouille. You can also boil them in salt water (like you would a potato) or eat them raw. This is when their artichoke-like flavor is strongest. The many diverse ways to prepare and enjoy Jerusalem artichokes are one of the culinary benefits of this plant.

REGROW-CHECK

Light ✽✽✽
Warmth ✽✽
Humidity ✽✽
Difficulty ✽

ONIONS

The onion is probably one of the few plants in the world that has brought everyone to tears at least once. Nevertheless, it is indispensable in our kitchens and adds a tasty kick to many dishes.

Onions are among the longest cultivated plants in the world. They have been part of human history for a whopping 5,000 years. Even the ancient Egyptians and Greeks appreciated the power of onions: rich in vitamins, easy to grow, and easy to store. They have really stood the test of time.

Their long history in many regions all over world explain why there are so many different types of onions. They vary in size, color, shape, spiciness, and country of origin. Even to this day, onions are the most widely cultivated vegetables worldwide. Nutritionally speaking, onions are very high in calcium and vitamin C, all while being low in calories with just 40 calories per 3½oz. (100g).

The heaviest onion ever grown weighed a whopping 11lbs (5kg). Unfortunately, you won't be able to achieve this with your regrown version (and if you do, you have magic gardening powers). Nevertheless, onions regrow very easily, so get the tissues ready.

Tissue alert! Your eyes tear when cutting onions because of an amino acid containing sulfur and an enzyme called alliinase. Both substances exist in the onion's cells, but they only come into contact with each other when the onion is cut. These two substances create an irritant when they meet. And that's what makes us get so "emotional."

REGROW YOUR ONION

1 Remove the lower part of the onion the same way you would if you were preparing to cook it. Don't cut too sparingly, however. The piece should be at least 1in (3cm) tall. Also, pay attention to the dried roots at the bottom. They need to stay intact for a healthy plant to regrow.

2 The underside of the onion doesn't need to be placed in water. Feel free to completely skip this step. Fresh roots will quickly grow in the same spot the dried roots are located.

3 The onion is an easygoing plant. Just place it in a container with slightly damp soil (the onion roots facing down) and cover it lightly with soil. Within a few weeks, the onions green sprouts will be coming up.

4 The onion itself won't completely grow back—at least never in my experience. But that's not a bad thing. You can use the onion sprouts as you would a scallion.

HARVESTING AND USE

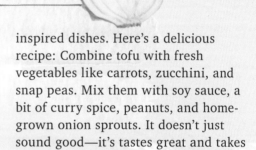

The sprouts of the regrown onion that grow from the onion stalk can be harvested. Be careful when harvesting so that the onion can continue to grow.

Have you ever tried onion sprouts? I think it's a great way to add a mild onion flavor to your dishes. To harvest, simply cut off individual "stems." I only ever take as much as I need at the time of harvesting for the food I'm making. This ensures that I always have fresh onions growing.

The onion sprouts can be eaten the same way as an onion itself: raw or cooked. I like to use them them in salads, especially in combination with crispy radishes and cucumber slices. Onion sprouts are also one of my favorite ingredients in Asian-inspired dishes. Here's a delicious recipe: Combine tofu with fresh vegetables like carrots, zucchini, and snap peas. Mix them with soy sauce, a bit of curry spice, peanuts, and home-grown onion sprouts. It doesn't just sound good—it's tastes great and takes very little time to make.

REGROW-CHECK

Light ✳✳✳
Warmth ✳✳
Humidity ✳✳
Difficulty ✳✳

BASIL

If I had to choose my favorite herb of all time, I think would probably be basil (sorry, mint, cilantro, chives, etc.!). There's nothing better than a basil leaf on top a plate of spaghetti with a classic tomato sauce or basil pesto with lots of pine nuts.

Basil, whose Latin name is *Ocimum basilicum*, belongs to the mint family. Even though we tend to instinctively associate Italy with basil, its origin is presumably a bit further east in India. The fact that basil ended up in warmer areas of the world when it spread, such as the Middle East, Egypt, and the Mediterranean region, tells us that our little green friend has an affection for warmth. The same applies to regrowing. In Northern Europe, the herb arrived during the Middle Ages. Today it's in gardens and on terraces and balconies everywhere.

Something that always shocks me is the short shelf-life of supermarket products. Who hasn't bought fresh basil only to see it wilt and die so soon after taking it home? Too often, the consequence of this is throwing out the basil and its plastic container to buy a new one—not very eco-friendly. Save your money by regrowing basil at home without much effort.

Fun Fact: The essential oil in basil, which is also responsible for its intense flavor, has an anti-inflammatory effect on the body. Basil is good for you, inside and out.

REGROW YOUR BASIL

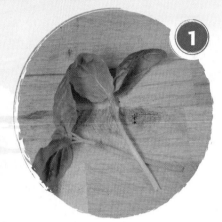

1 The first thing you need is fresh basil. Whether you get it from the supermarket or from somewhere else (a family member with a garden, for example) is totally up to you. Then, take several 2in (5cm) long pieces of the herb, and pluck off the lower leaves carefully. There should only be leaves at the top of the stem when you're done.

2 Place the small cuttings in a glass of water. The bottom of the stem should be in the water and the leaves should hang slightly out of the glass. Basil likes it bright and warm (but, please, not too warm; room temperature is fine). The water can be on the warmer side—this helps roots grow. A bright windowsill is the optimal location. You should change the water once every two to three days. Increased humidity also helps the basil plants grow its roots. If you want, you can place plastic wrap or a plastic bag with holes in it over the glass to increase humidity.

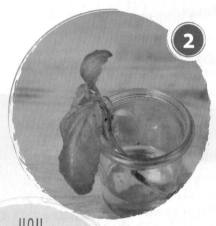

YOU DON'T ALWAYS HAVE TO USE A FLOWER POT

An equally chic and eco-friendly idea: old tin cans make great flower pots, especially for small plants like basil.

3 After two to three weeks, the roots of your basil cuttings should have grown significantly. Now you can plant them in a small container filled with soil. The roots should be completely covered by soil.

4 Make sure to water it regularly. Dry air causes the basil leaves to hang and stresses the plant. Slowly but surely your little kitchen herb will begin to grow more and more leaves.

HARVESTING AND USE

Harvesting your regrown basil is very simple: carefully pluck off the individual leaves. If the plant is a bit bigger, you might want to harvest a whole stem. However, a few leaves should always remain at the bottom of the plant. This will give the basil the strength to continue to grow more leaves. For big basil fans, it's probably a good idea to regrow multiple stems to make sure there's always enough basil on hand.

With this fresh herb, you can add a kick of basil to all sorts of dishes; be it pasta, pizza, or something else, basil always works.

REGROW-CHECK

Light ✳✳✳
Warmth ✳✳✳
Humidity ✳✳✳✳
Difficulty ✳✳

GALANGAL

→ Galangal is definitely one of the more unknown characters in this regrowing book. There are actually two different species hiding behind the name galangal—sounds complicated, but it is not.

✳

Galangal also makes a great decorative plant and is, therefore, a perfect regrow candidate. So, if you feel like exploring new culinary paths, the galangal (no matter which one you choose) is a great companion.

First there's the so-called lesser galangal (*Alpinia officinarum*), which is used mostly as a medicinal herb. Thai ginger (*Alpinia galanga*) is also often called galangal, but it used mostly as a spice in Southeast Asian cuisine. Both types belong to the ginger family. Visually, they are very similar. The underground shoot part of the plant is called a rhizome. And it's exactly this root we're after (the same goes for ginger and turmeric).

The type of galangal you choose is totally up to you. You'll be able to find Thai ginger pretty easily in specialty Asian cuisine stores. But be warned: regrowing galangal is only for the most patient of regrowers.

REGROW YOUR GALANGAL

1 It may be difficult to get your hands on some galangal in the first place. Asian specialty markets are a good place to start. Once you've successfully obtained one of the rhizomes, simply slice off a piece of it. Technically you could use the entire thing, but if you would like to save some to eat, a 1.5–2in (4–5cm) piece is all you need to start regrowing.

2 Choose a container that's not too small, so the galangal has room to grow. Place the rhizome piece in a trough about 2in (5cm) deep and cover it with soil. Now water the plant regularly and place it somewhere warm. Warmth is vital for the galangal.

RELOCATING
Your galangal will want to be repotted once ever one to three years.

3 Over time, the first sprouts and leaves will begin to appear. At this point, the plant doesn't just need heat, but also sunlight. As you can see, the galangal is a bit of a diva and spends a lot of time growing.

HARVESTING AND USE

As mentioned, growing galangal is the ultimate test in patience. Even in Southeast Asia—in the most optimal conditions—the ripening process of the rhizome takes around five years. Because most climates don't match these conditions, it can take significantly longer. But don't be sad; as I mentioned, galangal is a very pretty plant and can be a great aesthetic addition to your home.

How you use the galangal depends on the kind of galangal you've chosen. The spicy Thai-ginger is used mainly for Southeast Asian dishes. It's cut into thin slices for the classic hot and sour soup dish, tom yum. It's also a key ingredient in many Asian spice pastes. Its taste is similar to ginger.

The lesser galangal is used primarily for its medicinal healing power. It is especially good for digestion and has been used in this way in China for hundreds of years. It also helps stimulate your appetite.

REGROW-CHECK

Light ✳✳✳✳
Warmth ✳✳✳✳
Humidity ✳✳✳✳
Difficulty ✳✳✳✳✳

GINGER

Ginger has come to my rescue many many times. Whether stomach pains or a cold, fresh ginger tea often helps get rid of annoying discomforts. This is not just by chance—ginger is a well-known medicinal plant.

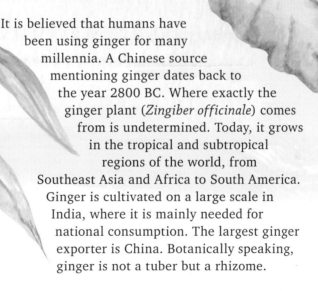

It is believed that humans have been using ginger for many millennia. A Chinese source mentioning ginger dates back to the year 2800 BC. Where exactly the ginger plant (*Zingiber officinale*) comes from is undetermined. Today, it grows in the tropical and subtropical regions of the world, from Southeast Asia and Africa to South America. Ginger is cultivated on a large scale in India, where it is mainly needed for national consumption. The largest ginger exporter is China. Botanically speaking, ginger is not a tuber but a rhizome.

✳

The leaves of the ginger plant have a very pretty, reed-like shape, and the blossom reminds me of tropical forests.

Even if you do not become a powerful ginger exporter, you can still regrow a beautiful plant out of this rhizome. So instead of buying an expensive decorative plant, just grow one out of a piece of ginger.

REGROW YOUR GINGER

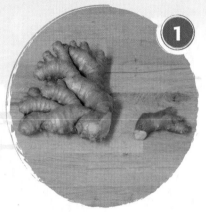

1 First, you need a piece of ginger. It doesn't have to be in the best shape. Younger rhizomes are better suited than older ones. The bigger the rhizome is, the quicker plants can develop out of it. For very fresh pieces, it's a good idea to let it dry out for a day or two. This should prevent any mold from developing.

2 Now you can place the ginger into some soil. Make sure to choose a large enough pot. Plant the ginger about 2in (5cm) deep and cover it with soil. Water the pot right away and place it somewhere warm. After a good two weeks, you should start to see the first sprouts.

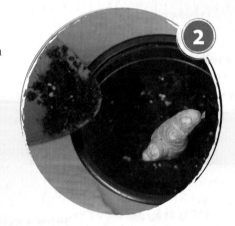

3 Once the sprouts appear, the location of the pot should not only be warm, but also bright, so that the plant can grow properly. Don't forget to water it! In the summer, you could also theoretically leave the ginger outside. Bring it in at night, however, if it's forcasted to be colder than 54°F (12°C).

HARVESTING AND USE

Harvesting fresh ginger can be difficult. Even in optimal conditions in the tropics and subtropics, it takes about eight months until harvest.

In any case, it makes a beautiful houseplant! Especially when this rhizome begins to put its exotic blossoms on display, the ginger plant can be a real eye-catcher.

By the way, in the winter it is normal for the plant to look wilted and as if it's dead. It will, however, begin to flourish again the following year. It's important that the plant doesn't get watered during this resting period. If the rhizome piece is very small, however, water it slightly so that it doesn't completely dry out.

Ginger, whether homegrown or purchased, can be used in a variety of ways. As mentioned, I often use it to make tea, especially in combination with mint or lemon. The spicy rhizome can also be used to make a refreshing homemade drink with lime, raspberry, and mint in mineral water. In the kitchen, ginger gives dishes that characteristic Asian flavor. It's especially good at lending its spice to soups: a carrot or pumpkin soup with coconut milk and ginger is a real treat.

REGROW-CHECK

Light ✳✳✳✳
Warmth ✳✳✳✳
Humidity ✳✳✳
Difficulty ✳✳✳✳

CORIANDER

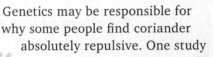 There's no middle ground when it comes coriander: either you love it or you hate it. I personally can't understand some people's extreme dislike of the herb. I am definitely a fan of coriander.

Genetics may be responsible for why some people find coriander absolutely repulsive. One study found that coriander haters had two genes that made coriander's "soapy taste" stand out; however, cultural factors also seem to play a role. If you grew up in a part of the world where coriander is often eaten and grown, you are much more likely to enjoy it. In areas where the leafy green herb isn't traditionally used, you're less likely to be a fan.

Regrowing coriander isn't rocket science. If you're a lover of coriander or attempting to become a new fan, you can get started regrowing coriander right away.

If you're someone who dislikes coriander, feel free to skip these instructions. Or maybe you'd like to give the herb a second chance? Sometimes you just have to get used to certain flavors.

This parsley family member likely originates from the Mediterranean region and has been growing there for a long time. Coriander seeds were found in the burial chamber of the Egyptian pharaoh Tutankhamen—a sign of its popularity at the time. It's one of the most widely used culinary herbs in the world.

REGROW YOUR CORIANDER

1 First, it's important to use fresh coriander that still has its roots intact. Individual stems can't be successfully regrown. Asian specialty markets often sell fresh coriander with its roots intact. Cut the leaves of the coriander 1–2in (2–4cm) above the root, and use it in the kitchen.

2 The remaining roots can now be placed in a glass of water for two to three days (the water should be changed every day). New sprouts will develop from the middle. Now the plant just needs a bright spot near a window.

3 After a quick stay in the glass of water, the coriander can be moved to the soil. Here it is very important that the air is humid, so something like a plastic bag, a plastic bottle with the bottom cut off, or a mini greenhouse should be placed over the plant. Don't forget to water it regularly. It may take a while until you have a fully-grown, bushy coriander plant in your home.

HARVESTING AND USE

As with other herbs, harvesting coriander leaves doesn't take much skill. You can carefully pluck individual leaves from a stem or cut off a whole stem; it all depending on how much you need. It's important to regularly water coriander because it loves humidity.

Now you can get started in the kitchen with your homegrown coriander. Classic Asian dishes especially receive their characteristic flavor because of these tasty leaves: soups, stir-fry vegetables, as well as heartier meals. From my own experience, I know that coriander is also very popular in Latin America. Along with avocados, tomatoes, onions, lime juice, salt, and pepper, cilantro (Spanish for coriander) is often added to guacamole because of its special flavor. I also love to use it in chili: plenty of tomato sauce, kidney beans, corn, chili, and, of course, coriander! Feel free to experiment with additional spices.

Of course, this herb is also very healthy: it's rich in vitamin A, vitamin C, calcium, and magnesium. Its medicinal properties are good for discomfort in the stomach and colon as well as for infections. Perhaps all these benefits are enough to change the mind of a skeptic or two?

REGROW-CHECK

Light ✳✳✳
Warmth ✳✳✳
Humidity ✳✳✳✳
Difficulty ✳✳✳

TURMERIC

Turmeric is known by many names: Gelbwurz, Gilbwurz, and saffron root. It belongs to the ginger family, which, based on its shape and size, is no surprise.

You can regrow turmeric at home with a bit of skill and patience. Like ginger, the beautiful turmeric leaves make this plant a wonderful decorative plant. Turmeric is only really demanding in terms of temperature, but more on that in the instructions.

The most obvious difference between ginger and turmeric is turmeric's rich orange color. Although it may look like a tuber, the botanical name for this part of the plant is a rhizome.

Turmeric is native to South Asia, or more specifically, India. There, this flashy rhizome is a common ingredient in the local cuisine. Typical Indian curry spice mixtures, for example, contain a large proportion of turmeric. Yellow root—the name says it all: it was used historically to dye paper and as a natural alternative the very expensive saffron. From India, the spice spread over time to southern Europe and reached Northern Europe in the Middle Ages.

In recent years, this yellow rhizome has gained a lot of popularity in the West. Turmeric is becoming standard in more and more household cookbooks, online recipes, and domestic spice racks. Although many find it to be very intense on its own, it gives a unique kick to many dishes, especially when combined with other herbs and spices.

REGROW YOUR TURMERIC

1 Tumeric rhizomes aren't available in most normal supermarkets, but can usually be found in Asian specialty stores or organic supermarkets. Then you can decide whether you want to plant the whole rhizome or just a piece of it. Generally, the bigger the piece, the easier it is for the plant to grow. If you decide to cut a piece off, let the surface of the cut dry for about a day before you plant it.

2 Now the turmeric can be planted in soil. Form a trough with your hand about 2in (5cm) deep to place the rhizome in. Cover it and water lightly. Permeable potting soil is best suited for this. Turmeric loves warmth, so look for the warmest part of your home to place the plant. Now it's time to wait!

YELLOW FINGERS

It's a good idea to wear disposable gloves when cutting and grating turmeric. This will save you from having dyed finger tips for the next couple of days.

3 After two to three weeks, you should see the first sprouts poke out of the soil. Now your turmeric plant will want to be somewhere with lots of sunlight. Over time, more and more leaves will grow and if you're lucky, in the right circumstances they might also blossom.

HARVESTING AND USE

I'm sure you can imagine it: a new tropical ambience in your home all thanks to this plant. If they blossom, you really do have a green thumb.

Technically, you can harvest the rhizome as soon as winter starts, but it's better to wait a year or so; then, the harvest will be really worth it. This is because rhizome formation doesn't really get going until the second year after being planted. If you plan to keep the plant for a long time, remember to use a larger flower pot.

In autumn, the leaves will slowly start to sag. You can overwinter the rhizome in the pot. They just need to be placed in a cooler location, like an unheated apartment stairwell or a chilly bedroom. You should water it much less in the winter as well. In the spring, you can begin to water more often (but not too much) and hope that the rhizome resumes sprouting.

Turmeric is great for soups, curries, and many other dishes. Let your creativity blossom!

REGROW-CHECK

Light ✲✲✲
Warmth ✲✲✲✲
Humidity ✲✲✲
Difficulty ✲✲✲✲

MINT

Mint is certainly not an herb whose fame recently came into fashion. On the contrary, this fragrant herb has always been a hit. Charlemagne cultivated mint in his empirical gardens.

The origin of mint cannot be pinpointed to one specific region. Its native land is the entire northern hemisphere. It is most comfortable in temperate climates.

The story of how mint came to be is described in Greek mythology. The river god Kokyrus had a beautiful daughter named Minthe. Hades, the god of the underworld, fell in love with her. The goddess Perseophone, the wife of Hades, was not amused by this at all and killed Minthe as a result. As if the murder itself wasn't enough, she tore the young woman into many pieces. A sad Hades collected all of Minthe's remains and spread them on the sunny slope of a mountain. A bushel of mint grew from each piece. Although this story is pretty cruel, it is true that mint is a very good vegetative propagator, making it a perfect candidate for regrowing.

It's easy to care for this weed-like herb—you should have no problem regrowing mint.

Its name is likely a derivation of the word *menta*, the Latin name it was given during Roman times. Even back then, there were many varieties of mint: Today we know of more than 20 different species of Mint. Mint gives its name to its plant family. Other plants in the mint family include rosemary, lavender, and thyme.

REGROW YOUR MINT

1 First, you need some mint. If you want to buy some in the supermarket, make sure you buy the freshest you can find. The first step is to cut off a few of the mint stems. The stems, ideally 3–4in (7–10cm) long can be reused. Remove the leaves at the bottom of the stem so that there are only leaves at the top.

2 Leave the mint tips in a glass of water for seven to ten days. A sunny and warm location will help your new plants grow. After that, it's off to the soil (you should be able to see the roots beginning to form at this point). Technically, you could also skip the water and place the stems directly in soil. In this case, however, it's important to place something like a plastic bag with holes over the plant in order to increase humidity.

A BREATH OF FRESH HERB

Because mint helps maintain fresh breath, it is used in almost every toothpaste, mouthwash, and chewing gum—what a useful herb!

3 Planting mint is very easy. There is nothing in particular that you need to pay attention to. It is better, however, if you use special cultivation soil. This will help your mint stems grow roots. Don't forget to water them! Your mint will be especially happy in a bright and warm location; a slightly shady location is also okay. If you want to grow a lot of mint, it makes sense to grow it outside.

HARVESTING AND USE

After a few weeks, you will have lush mint leaves. Cut off individual stems close to the soil and use them for whatever you like. The plants will begin to sprout again very quickly, so feel free to take a lot at once. Mint is most aromatic when it's fresh.

I really like it in combination with fruits, especially with strawberries and dark chocolate—it's a dream! Other, more exotic fruits, like mango, make interesting combinations as well. For real mint fans, I recommend using it in smoothies. Especially in the summer, mint gives drinks a refreshing kick. You might recognize this refreshing kick as a key ingredient in mojitos, which just wouldn't be the same without mint. Mint leaves are a big hit in non-alcoholic drinks as well. My recommendation: mint with raspberry and ginger—this combination is especially good in the summer. In the winter, you can simply use it to make yourself a cup of tea. As you can see, there are lots of possibilities.

REGROW-CHECK

Light ✳✳
Warmth ✳✳
Humidity ✳✳✳✳
Difficulty ✳✳

LEMONGRASS

Although the name of this vegetable contains the word lemon, it is not related to the citrus fruit, except in taste. It belongs to the grass family. Most often, this West Indian grass ends up being added to ingredients in a pot.

It is still unclear where lemon grass actually originates from. Some experts believe that *Cymbopogon citratus* (its botanical name) might originate in the southern regions of India or Sri Lanka. In Asia, lemongrass has long been a staple ingredient of many dishes, and is also used occasionally as a medicinal herb. Especially in Thai, Vietnamese, and Indonesian cuisine, this lemon-tasting grass is seen in pots and woks.

There are surprisingly many varieties of lemongrass: about 55 different types. For use in the kitchen, the so-called West Indian lemongrass is the most common. The East Indian variant is primarily used as a medicinal herb and for creating perfumes. The smell is probably its most striking feature, next to its flavor of course: fresh tangy lemon.

In its native region, lemongrass grows in large bushels that can get up to 3–7ft (1–2m) tall, making it a real giant of a plant. But don't worry; it won't get that big in your home.

Only the stems are used for cooking and you can regrow these at home!

REGROW YOUR LEMONGRASS

1 Remove the upper two-thirds of a bundle of lemongrass stalks. You only need the bottom part for regrowing, which should be about 2–3in (5–7cm) long.

2 Place the lemongrass heads into a water bath. The water in the container should cover the lower part of the stems. The end you removed the tips from should be sticking out of the glass and not underwater. Lemongrass like bright and warm environments. A bright window in your house should do. You should change the water every two to three days. If you wished, you could skip the water and plant the stems in the soil right away.

3 If you've chosen the water method, you'll begin to see new roots on the stems after one to two weeks. Once there are many new roots and the root system seems to be healthy, you can plant the lemongrass in soil. Make sure most of the lemongrass is above the surface of the soil.

4 Placing your lemongrass in a bright and warm area is still important. Also remember to water regularly. After a few weeks, the grass will have grown significantly and can reach a height of 12in (30cm) or more.

HARVESTING AND USE

Once the stalks have grown enough, you can harvest the upper third of your regrown lemongrass. To do this, carefully cut off as many stalks as you need. Make sure to always use a knife that is clean and sharp. You need to be careful that you don't accidentally uproot an entire stalk. If you follow all these tips, your lemongrass will continue to grow happily after harvesting. Now you'll always have fresh sprouting lemon aroma on hand and an exotic flair in your home—what a gift!

To use it, you can take a look in many Asian cuisine cookbooks or in online forums. The possibilities for using this tasty, tender, lemon-smelling herb in all sorts of dishes are enormous. Whether it's vegetable stir fry with soy sauce, slightly spicy Thai salad, or soup, this grass gives any dish that special something. Don't feel limited to food! You can also make a refreshing lemonade with lemongrass as a refreshing summer drink.

With regrown lemongrass you'll always have an exotic spice in the house, which will definitely motivate you to try out recipes from far away cultures.

REGROW-CHECK

Light ★★★★
Warmth ★★★★
Humidity ★★★
Difficulty ★★★

PINEAPPLE

For me, the pineapple is the queen of the tropics. Its shape, smell, and, of course, its taste are truly unique. I bet that those that claim to not like pineapple have just never tasted one that's perfectly ripe and fresh.

Pineapples are very high-maintenance fruits to regrow, considering the amount of warmth and light they need. Even under optimal conditions (e.g., in a very bright winter garden) it is almost impossible to grow a proper pineapple in the northern regions of the world. Nonetheless, pineapple stems can be a beautiful decorative plant for your home.

I often found pineapples from the supermarket to be disappointing. For this reason, it's worth it to spend a bit more money and buy one from a fresh fruit stand or shop. The tastiest ones are probably found in the countries where pineapple is grown. The main pineapple growing regions are India, Indonesia, Thailand, the Philippines, Brazil, and Costa Rica.

Originally, pineapples come from South America. According to experts, various tribes have been successfully cultivating pineapples there, especially in the tropical regions of the continent, for 4,000 years. After taking over the Americas, pineapple was spread to the rest of the world mainly by the Spanish and Portuguese. The cultivation of pineapples was then heavily promoted in other colonial territories such as India and Southeast Asia. In Europe, wealthy families enjoyed the exclusive and novel fruit. For many people, the fruit first became attainable in the 20th century—initially mostly as a canned good.

REGROW YOUR PINEAPPLE

1 Twist out the stem of the pineapple. This works best with an already ripened pineapple. Be careful not to damage the leaves in the process. If you notice that you can't remove the stem by twisting, you can remove the upper quarter of the pineapple with a knife, and then cut the remaining fruit flesh away from the base of the stem. If there are additional leaves very close to the bottom of the stem, you should carefully remove these as well.

2 Then, place the stem and leaves in water. The location is very important here: bright, very warm, and very humid. A warmer and bright winter garden or a window would be well suited. Above all, heat is important for developing roots. The water should be regularly changed. After about a week, you should begin to see the first roots growing out of the stalk.

3 Once a few roots are clearly visible, it's time to plant! For this, there isn't anything special to consider. With a lot of light, warmth, and humidity, the pineapple will bring some tropical flair to your home.

HARVESTING AND USE

In non-tropic regions, it is very difficult to harvest a whole pineapple. Under optimal conditions, more and more leaves will grow from the center of the leaf stem and, after a few years, you may see a mini-pineapple emerge from the center.

Because pineapples are so extremely sensitive to cold, it is not easy to regrow a pineapple to the point where it produces fruit. The plant itself is very decorative, however, even without the regrowing fruit. Currently, there are decorative pineapple plants for sale that include a small pineapple fruit, but the one you regrow yourself with effort and love will be much more meaningful.

Pineapples are rich in vitamin A and C as well as calcium, magnesium, and iron. Unless you're a fan of Hawaiian pizza, you'll probably eat the fruit raw. Although: Cooked pineapple also goes very well with Asian curries. I especially enjoy it as in a smoothie or juiced in combination with papaya or mango.

REGROW-CHECK

Light ★★★★
Warmth ★★★★★
Humidity ★★★★
Difficulty ★★★★★

AVOCADO

Life without avocados? I can't even imagine it. Their buttery consistency and their taste that pairs well with so many dishes—definitely one of my weekly staples. And it's so healthy!

It will only be possible to harvest your own avocado fruit with a lot of luck and the best conditions (for example, in a greenhouse or winter garden). In the tropics, it takes four whole years before a tree begins to bear fruit. But even if your avocado tree won't bear any fruit, you'll still end up with a beautiful houseplant.

In recent years, avocados have become a hit food in the West. Every supermarket stocks them these days. There are even restaurants entirely centered on avocados. In addition to its very mild taste, avocados are also nice to look at: their deep green color together with their creamy texture is one of a kind.

There's no debating that avocados are native to Southern Mexico. From Central America, the Spaniards spread the green berry (botanically speaking, it is one) to the south of the continent. In Chile and Peru, they're still grown widely today. These days, avocados are grown in many topical countries all over the world, and you can even find them growing in the southernmost part of Spain.

You've probably guessed it already: avocados like it warm! Nevertheless, it's possible for those of us in cooler climates to grow avocados at home as well. Because the new plant will grow from the seed, it's the most important part of the avocado to regrowers.

REGROW YOUR AVOCADO

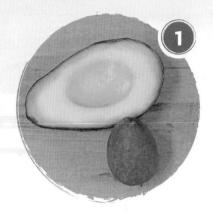

1 Gently remove the avocado seed, wash it thoroughly under cold water, and dry it off. Using four toothpicks, poke holes into the seed at even distances apart. Poke the holes slightly below the middle half of the seed. Be careful not to prick your finger.

2 Place your toothpick-avocado seed construction on a small glass of water. The toothpicks ensure that only the lower part of the seed is submerged in water. A bright and warm location is important. Also make sure to regularly change the water.

3 After a few weeks, you will start to see roots growing from the bottom of the seed. Eventually, the tip of the seed will break open and a small stalk will emerge. Continue to change the water regularly and give the plant some time. After a few weeks, you will begin to see the first leaves.

4 Once the plant is 6–8in (15–20cm) tall, you can plant it in soil. Make sure that everything but the top of the seed is covered in soil. A bright area and regular watering will help your avocado continue to grow.

REGROW GIFT

A home-grown avocado plant makes the perfect gift. What is better than a present made with care and love?

HARVESTING AND USE

As mentioned, you probably won't be able to regrow your own avocados with a regrown avocado plant. Unfortunately, most climatic conditions aren't right. That being said, you'll get a really great houseplant from a seed that you would probably otherwise throw away.

Sometimes, no roots will grow out of the seed. For this reason, it's a good idea to regrow two or three seeds at once. This increases your chances of success.

Avocados are, of course, very healthy. In particular, their unsaturated fatty acids are very useful for people who eat mainly vegetables and don't consume much fat in their diet. Many people are surprised at the calorie count of avocados, but this is unnecessary. With about 200 calories per 4 ounces, the avocado is one of the most

calorie-dense fruits; however, this is healthy as long as you don't overdo it. Here, too, the the motto "everything in moderation" applies. Also, from an ecological point of view, avocados have to travel far and wide to get to our supermarkets, and they require a lot of water to grow. So be sure to savor them!

REGROW-CHECK

Light ✳✳✳
Warmth ✳✳✳✳
Humidity ✳✳✳
Difficulty ✳✳✳

MANGO

The smell of mango immediately makes me think of vacation. Especially when vacationing in Southeast Asia or Hawaii, you'll often run into this exotic fruit: sometimes in the form of a creamy lassi (a type of yogurt drink) or as a spicy side salad.

No matter how you prepare it, the sweet, fruity mango is always a hit—as long as the fruit is ripe. As with many other fruits, the proper ripeness is crucial for the mango's delicious flavor. You can tell that a mango is ripe when it yields to firm, yet gentle pressure. Your nose can help as well: ripe mangoes exude an intense aroma. For most of the types of mangoes found in supermarkets, they will also have a yellowish-red color when ripe.

In other parts of the world, there are many different types of mangoes. They come in different shapes, sizes, and colors. Especially in India, mangoes are an indispensable part of culinary life—and that's no coincidence. The mango originates from the region between modern day India and Myanmar.

Today, the fruit grows worldwide in tropical areas. Nevertheless, India is still the undisputed number one producer of mangoes. China, Thailand, Pakistan, and Mexico follow suit. Mangoes also grow in the US and in parts of Australia.

You can join the club of mango tree growers. All you need is a healthy mango seed and (of course) patience. You'll be rewarded with a wonderful ornamental plant, but you will most likely be unable to produce fruit in northern regions.

REGROW YOUR MANGO

1 Cut open a ripe mango and remove the seed pouch. But don't throw it away: this is exactly what you need to regrow your mango. To get to the seeds, pry open the seed pouch carefully with a knife. This is best done at the top of the pod (where the mango's stem was). After a little prodding, you should be able to open them and find the kidney-shaped seeds.

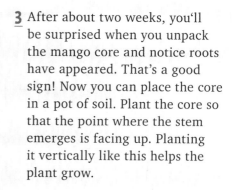

2 The mango core doesn't need to be placed in water. Covering it in a wet towel is more than enough. Wrap the core in a clean, damp kitchen towel. This kitchen towel package can then be placed in a freezer bag and sealed. Let it sit for 10 to 14 days and the core will do all the work.

3 After about two weeks, you'll be surprised when you unpack the mango core and notice roots have appeared. That's a good sign! Now you can place the core in a pot of soil. Plant the core so that the point where the stem emerges is facing up. Planting it vertically like this helps the plant grow.

HARVESTING AND USE

Over time, a real mango tree will begin to grow and give your home an exotic flair. The tree will not bear fruit. It is generally too cold in North America for this plant, and even under very good conditions, it's almost impossible to grow mango fruits indoors. Nevertheless, I find it fascinating to see how a decorative tree can be grown in just a few months from a core that would have otherwise been thrown in the trash.

Even if you probably won't wind up with any self-grown mangoes in your kitchen, these tasty fruits can be eaten many different ways. I like them best raw in a fruit salad. Very ripe mangoes can also be used for smoothies or lassis. Mangoes go great together with other fruits, and even vegetables like spinach. It can also be served warm, which is especially common with South Asian curries. In India, mangoes are seen as a medicinal fruit that have symbolic meaning. This is why the mango is the national fruit of India, as well as Pakistan and the Philippines.

LOCATION PREFERENCE

This probably comes as no surprise: mangoes like it warm and bright; they also appreciate being watered regularly.

REGROW-CHECK

Light ✶✶✶✶
Warmth ✶✶✶✶✶
Humidity ✶✶✶✶
Difficulty ✶✶✶✶

WHEN THINGS DON'T GO AS PLANNED: PREVENTING PROBLEMS

As always in life, sometimes things just don't go as hoped, despite the best planning. This chapter will help you avoid common mistakes, and teach you how to react accordingly to problems you might face along the way. The tips are organized by problems with pests and pathogens, as well as problems involving cultivating and caring for your plants.

PROBLEMS WITH PESTS
AND PATHOGENS

This section deals with the bullies of the plant world, fungi and microorganisms. The best way to prevent an infestation is by growing your plants under the best conditions to make them resilient, instead of having to fight off unwanted guests after the fact.

Rot

Rot is a pretty common problem in regrowing. This is because we often cut off a part of the plant. In this wounded area, rot can sometimes occur and spread. If your regrown plant is affected, you should generously remove the rotting piece and let the new cut dry. Then you can return the plant to its water glass or soil. Sometimes, a case of rot means the end of your vegetable. For example, if the roots of a spring onion are rotten—very soft spots and a strong odor are strong signs of rot—then it belongs in the garbage.

Additional tips to prevent rot:

* Only regrow healthy plants.

* Always wash regrow vegetables thoroughly with tap water before you place them in a glass of water or flower pot.

* For the water method, be sure to change the water almost daily.

* Always work cleanly and disinfect your tools with alcohol if you can.

* Sterilize your soil in the oven at 400°F (205°C) for 30 minutes and let it cool (you can also sterilize your soil in the microwave).

* If you're using a mini greenhouse, ventilate it regularly.

If the rot is very advanced, the plant can no longer be saved.

Mold

Mold and other fungal pathogens are not something you want to have sitting in your kitchen. Your plants aren't big fans of them either, so you should take all necessary precautions. The cause of these unpleasant diseases is usually improper care. The main culprit: low-quality potting soil. This is because it can become a perfect breeding ground for mold at high humidity. It's advisable to invest in good soil to save yourself a lot of work and worry. Ideally, you should use high-quality potting soil or coconut coir. These are best suited because they're particularly low in germs.

Additional tips against mold:

* Constantly wet soil promotes mold growth, so don't over-water.

* Peat pots are especially susceptible to mold (the remedy is less watering and sufficient air circulation)—apart from the fact that they should be avoided in hobby gardening for ecological reasons.

* If you're using a mini greenhouse, ventilate it regularly.

This avocado seed unfortunately suffered from waterlogging.

Mildew

Mildew is one of the most common fungal diseases in plants and has cost many gardeners their nerves, time, and, ultimately, their harvest. When regrowing, mildew can also be an issue under certain conditions. Generally, we differentiate between downy mildew and powdery mildew. Downy mildew can especially occur if you're regrowing in a mini greenhouse. You can tell if your plant is suffering from downy mildew if it is developing a fungal film (a whitish coating) on the underside of the leaf. You can prevent mildew by making sure that the parts of the plant above the soil stay dry. Mildew loves wet leaves.

Additional tips to prevent mildew:

* Avoid using mini greenhouses with a flat cover. With these models, condensation forms inside the greenhouse winds up dripping directly onto the plants.

* Don't spray your plants with too much water from a spray bottle; this well-intended technique often does more harm than good.

* Preventively, you can spray your regrow vegetables with horsetail extract from special retailers. Its natural ingredients strengthen the plant's defenses. Don't use chemical pesticides because you will want to eat the vegetables shortly thereafter.

Aphids

An aphid infestation aren't especially appealing when it involves our food. These small insects are particularly prone to attack weakened plants. Unfortunately, our newly regrown friends fall into this category. Making new roots costs the little plants lots of energy and weakens them. So, aphids have it easy. If one of your plants is attacked by aphids, first separate it from any other regrow plants around it.

Aphids literally weigh down your chances of successful regrowing.

Most of the time, wiping the leaves clean of the insects with a damp cloth is enough (a bit of bubbly mild soap won't hurt either—aphids excrete a sticky substance).

Additional tips against aphids:
(These strategies are only useful for large quantities.)

* For a strong infestation, a natural spray made from neem is helpful. This can usually be found in specialty gardening stores.

* Beneficial insects like ladybugs and their larvae can help keep aphids in check—whether or not you want them flying around your house is another question.

Gnats

These small insects look like typical fruit flies that can often be found fluttering around the kitchen. They like to stay close to soil and lay their eggs there. The gnat larvae are the real problem because they eat organic material like roots. A mature plant won't be too affected by them. For regrown plants, however, this root eating is very problematic and can cause the untimely death of your new plant.

GNATS OR FRUIT FLIES

You can easily fight these pesky insects with adhesive traps from a gardening store. You can determine which insect you're dealing with using a small trick: fill a glass with a mixture of vinegar, water, and some dish soap. If the little things fly into the glass, they're fruit flies and not gnats.

Additional tips against gnats:

* You can prevent them by using high-quality soil (preferably peat-free and organic).

* Sterilize your soil, especially if it's cheap soil (see page 120).

* You can delay the development of the larvae by keeping the soil a bit dryer.

* The most effective way to combat gnats is with a beneficial insect called steinernema feltiae, a predatory nematode that you can order online.

Gnats can become a real scourge.

CULTIVATION PROBLEMS

If conditions aren't exactly suitable, your seedlings may have trouble getting started. Here you will learn how to counteract certain symptoms.

Etiolation

Etiolation is when plant stems grow unusually long, which makes the stem soft and weak over time. This instinctual growth happens when the plant is trying everything it can to reach the light it needs but isn't currently getting. In the worst cases, the stems get so long that the weight of the leaves becomes too heavy to hold up and the plant collapses. To avoid etiolation, location is key. The simplest solution is, of course, to increase the amount of light that the plant is getting. For example, you could move the plant from near a window facing north to a window facing south.

Additional tips against etiolation:

* You can stabilize an etiolating plant by attaching it to a wooden skewer; this is only a temporary solution and does not stop etiolation from lack of light.

* If the temperature requirements of the plant allow for it, you can cool the plant if you notice etiolation; plants curb their metabolism and, therefore, seek less sun when they're cold.

* Plants should be placed directly by a window and not in the middle of the room. Even if it appears bright enough, our eyes cannot detect the intensity of the sunlight that plants require.

With etiolation, plants waste a lot of energy trying to grow tall and compensate for the lack of light.

Sunburn

It may surprise you, but yes, plants can also get a sunburn. Even plants that originally come from tropical regions and are very used to strong sunlight can get a sunburn. This can set back their growth by weeks. If they're not getting the proper level of sunlight for a while, they lose their built-in sunscreen. So, if you want to place your regrow babies in the garden or on the deck (weather permitting), then they shouldn't get direct sunlight immediately. Let the plants get used to the sun for at least one or two weeks—first in full shade, then somewhere partly shady, and finally in direct sunlight.

Additional tips against sunburn:

* When you're slowly introducing the plant to sun, you should especially avoid direct sunlight at midday. This is the part of the day where the sun is the most intense.

* If there are no shady places for your plant, you can shade your plants. A white fleece, which is actually used to protect against frost in the spring, is perfect for this.

* Whatever you do, don't place a closed mini greenhouse in direct sunlight; the high temperatures that would develop inside would likely kill the plant.

Chlorosis

Chlorosis is the result of chlorophyll deficiency in plants and can be considered a type of malnourishment. Usually it is due to a lack of iron or nitrogen. These are the nutrients required to create the green leaf color. Without green chlorophyll, plants can't engage in photosynthesis to survive. You can recognize chlorosis by the fact that the leaves turn yellow and eventually die off. Even if your plant is only lacking specific nutrients, you should still balance the deficiency with a complete fertilizer that contains all necessary micro- and macronutrients.

Additional tips against chlorosis:

* Mineral liquid fertilizers are best for quickly eliminating chlorosis because the nutrients can be directly absorbed by the plant.

* If the fertilizer contains iron chelate (see fertilizer label), this can be absorbed very well by plants.

* Foliar fertilizers can also quickly replenish a lack of nutrients, but not all fertilizers are suitable for this. Make sure to only use foliar fertilizers that have been proven to work. With foliar fertilization, the fertilizer isn't poured into the soil but sprayed directly onto the leaves.

Lack of rooting

So, you followed the instructions exactly, completed all the steps correctly, but your regrow plants refuse to root? There are many possible reasons for this. For one thing, it may be that the plant was already too old and not healthy enough to grow roots; old and shriveled plants are unlikely to grow new roots. It could also be due to low temperatures. Try to grow the plants in an environment at or above 68°F (20°C). It can also be helpful to try different propagation methods. If the water glass method doesn't work very well, try planting your regrow plant directly in potting soil.

Additional tips for lack of rooting:

* Placing a styrofoam plate under the water glass, pot, or mini greenhouse prevents warmth from escaping underneath the plant. This keeps the plants warmer overall.

* Very passionate regrowers may want to purchase a heating pad with a thermostat to make sure the plants are always at the perfect temperature for rooting. Not only does this increase the success rate, it also speeds up the growing process.

* Be patient and do not consistently work with plants in the rooting phase; by removing the stems to check for roots, sensitive replacement tissues are destroyed, which the plant needs to create new roots.

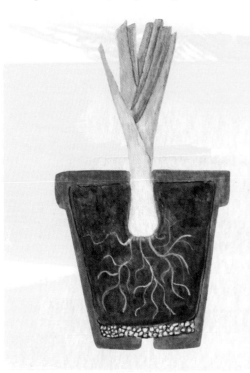

RESOURCES

 Need book tips or online resources? On the following pages you can find all kinds of useful information. Have fun regrowing—and eating!

ADDITIONAL READING

Books

Bartholomew, Mel. *Square Meter Gardening*.
Frances Lincoln Publishers, 2013.

Harrison, John. *Low-Cost Living: Live Better, Spend Less*.
Right Way, 2009.

Harrison, John. *Vegetable, fruit and herb growing in small spaces*.
Robinson, 2010.

RHS (Hrsg.). *Vegetables and Fruit in Pots: Simple Steps to Success*.
DK, 2012.

Warren, Piers und Pettingell, Tessa. *How to Store Your Garden Produce. The Key to Self-Sufficiency. 2nd Edition*.
Green Books, 2008.

Internet

www.plantura.garden
The online garden magazine of the authors. Here you'll find helpful tips about growing vegetables, herbs, and fruit.

www.blissfulbasil.com
A great site for veggie dishes: The recipes range from simple classics to elaborate creations.

www.deliciouslyella.com
This site from Ella Woodward is a favorite. The recipes are usually very easy, taste great, and look great on your plate, too.

www.inthemakingbybelen.com/food
The most visually appealing vegan dishes you can imagine.

www.ohmyveggies.com
This site is full of colorful recipes, but not all of them are vegan. It's a great place for those getting started with healthy dieting.

INDEX

ABOUT THE AUTHORS

This book is a collaborative project based on the joy of regrowing, writing, and gardening in general. Motivating more people to live a healthier life and be closer to nature (especially city people like us) is what drives us. Above all, we hope that young people will have fun learning about regrowing and experiencing their own miracles of nature.

A brief note about the authors: Felix and I have known each other for many years and share a passion for all things green. Even before he started his higher education, Felix started a company called *Pflanzenspezl* ("The Plant Buddy" in English), which distributed old and rare fruit trees all over Europe. In 2017, we both founded Plantura, a digital gardening magazine that provides high-quality content to a large community of home gardeners. While Felix contributes real plant expertise and business knowledge, I manage the writing and my fascination for all things green.

We hope that this book brings joy to all who read it, and we hope it leads to more green foods to eat inside your own four walls.

Right: Melissa is the writer and Felix is the plant expert.

PHOTO CREDITS

Front cover: Plantura GmbH
Title page: Plantura GmbH

Photos coutersy Shuttertstock: On SET, 15; Jukov studio, 23; smspsy, 26; vaivirga, 128; Pixel-Shot, 129; Thannaree Deepul, 131

All other photos are from Plantura GmbH

Illustrations by Johanna Seibel